SIMPLE LIVING
Right Now
Ending Life's Chaos & Reclaiming Joy

BRYNN BURGER

Simple Living Right Now: Ending Life's Chaos and Reclaiming Joy

© 2019 Brynn Burger

Praise for
Simple Living RIGHT NOW

"In a sea of books about simplifying your life, *Simple Living Right Now* is a clear stand out. Brynn's sense of humor shines through beautifully. It is like getting advice from a friend in the business instead of feeling like you are in class. She makes you feel like you want to invite her over for coffee to show off your organized house. You will be so thankful for the peace Brynn's practical steps will bring to your mind and to your home."

-Qat Wanders, Best-Selling Author

"Simple Living RIGHT NOW walks the reader through reclaiming joy and order in their life, step-by-step. From re-gifting the Fiestaware to paring down the closet, Brynn's writing is equal parts life coach and drill instructor. Brynn just gets it. Her book helps us peel away the chaos that often overwhelms each of us and get right to the heart of our emotions. She exposes her own shortcomings in order to make us accept our

own. Each sentence is loud and powerful in a hushed, accepting tone."

Simple Living Right Now is a realistic guide to decluttering and creating the simple life that you've been longing for. Using loads of humor and wit, Brynn shows you how to let go of fear and unload the stuff that has been weighing you down. With five easy-to-follow steps, you will find that a less chaotic life is within reach."

"*Simple Living Right Now* will give your spirit a much needed lift no matter where you currently are in life. In the chaotic world we all navigate daily, there's never much time to sit and just be. That's because our world revolves around stuff; stuff on our to-do lists, stuff on our calendars, stuff in our homes. Brynn shows us in simple and inviting steps how to simplify our lifestyles to allow for joy to make a return entrance. Her tone is warm and welcoming; her approach gentle and non-judgmental. When you finish reading this book you'll find yourself asking, "what took me so long?"

 -Lisa Leshaw, therapist and mental health advocate

To my incredible, adventure-seeking husband who never batted an eyelash when I pitched the idea to live tiny and who has been cheering me on with the same ferocity everyday since we met. I would not be the best version of myself without you by my side.

And to Briggs and Sparrow, our two wild kiddos who are extreme in every good and wonderful and crazy sense of the word. I wasn't always convinced I wanted to be a wife, but I never doubted I'd someday be a mama. Thank you for making that dream come true.

Simple Living RIGHT NOW
Ending Life's Chaos & Reclaiming Joy

Foreword

Carl Jung, the Swiss psychiatrist and psychoanalyst, is credited with saying, "Who looks outside, dreams; who looks inside, awakes." Isn't that what we all want? We all want to experience our own great awakening. Beyond living the dreams we want to be present in the now.

Brynn was living her dream – the house, the husband, the kids, and the income. But each day she was finding herself buried deeper and deeper in frustration and emotional fatigue. With bills mounting from every direction this mother was prepared to get extreme! She is no stranger to the extreme either.

As a parent to an extreme son (medically diagnosed with a myriad of behavioral disorders), she and her husband knew they needed to awaken and they quickly realized it would take a grand gesture. By downsizing their life, their space, their consumption, and all that comes with it, they began to find relief and release. Now Brynn is sharing that extreme act of self-love, if you will, with readers around the globe.

You don't have to be the parent of an extreme child. You don't have to be surrounded by mountains of debt. You don't even have to be addicted to HGTV, to learn from her sage advice. What you do need though is a desire to WAKE UP!

Simple Living Right Now walks the reader through reclaiming joy and order in their life, step-by-step. From re-gifting the Fiestaware to paring down the closet, Brynn's writing is equal parts life coach and drill instructor.

There is a time to nurture and a time to be proactive and Simple Living Right Now is the only true guide to walking that tightrope!

- Andrew M. Odom, founder and editor of Tiny r(E)volution

Introduction
Our Journey Toward Simplicity

"We have some say over the size of our lives ..."

-Shawna Nyquist, Presence Over Perfect

*Cue my best impression of my teenage crush, Will Smith, circa 1992.

Now this is a story all about how
My life got flipped, turned upside down.
And I'd like to take a minute, just sit right there,
I'll tell you how I became the mom with the
messy bun hair.

It's true, friends. Almost three years ago, I found myself sitting on our couch, nursing our newest bundle of tears and dirty diapers, surrounded by a threatening pile of laundry, watching our completely wild then four-year-old son running crazy through our farmhouse.

Like any good mother on her maternity leave, I was crying my way through binge watching seasons of shows on HGTV when an episode of something featuring tiny houses came on. I don't know if the laundry avalanched over the remote or I was just too tired to notice, but that week I ended up watching an entire series of shows about tiny living.

The idea of living in a house that was 400 square feet or smaller wasn't entirely foreign to my husband and me since our first home was only 600 square feet, including the loft. However, this wasn't 2006. Now we had two kids. Just packing for a trip with them felt like it required a U-Haul. How could we possibly downsize 2200 square feet of farmhouse and 15 acres of stuff into such minimal real estate?

The people featured on these tiny house shows looked like super hip, mega trendy, entrepreneurial singles or newly-engaged twentysomethings with all of their dreams before them and the road with their little 120-square-foot tiny houses on wheels. I mean, could two midwestern kind of farmer, kind of hippie parents *actually* sell their stuff and move their kids into a small house or would they all perish in the struggle?

It was in that moment of spit-up covered glory that we made our decision to downsize and live simply. Yeah, we go big ... errrrrrr, uhhhhhh tiny.

Trained for Trials

Our little family was not immune to terrifying adversity. Just a few years before, my husband and I and our over 30 combined years of experience working with at-risk youth and children with disabilities began to realize our oldest child was showing signs of behavior disorders. Fast-forward through three-and-a-half years of judgment, specialists, therapy appointments, and impossible decisions, and we knew we needed to figure out a way for one of us to stay home to teach him because public school was not working alongside his diagnoses.

At that time, we had a newborn daughter whose time in the NICU left us buried in debt, a mortgage to what we had imagined was our dream home but made us so house-poor we couldn't enjoy it, and a son who needed more care than we could financially provide for him.

So, like the professional nerd I am, I began to research. In the year that followed that exact moment, I consumed every article, medical journal, sciency-book, Pinteresty-pin, and blogger board available that covered the correlation of simple living and kids like ours.

The research was in and all reports supported reducing the stimulation of what we call "extreme children". Our son officially has a diagnosis of severe, combined ADHD (Attention Deficit Hyperactivity Disorder)—both the inattentive and hyperactive varieties, GAD (Generalized Anxiety Disorder), SPD (Sensory Processing Disorder), ODD (Oppositional Defiant Disorder), and what is called 2e (Twice Exceptional) meaning that he is academically gifted but emotionally deficient.

All of those acronyms, simply put, meant we spent every single day living with a tiny ticking time bomb.

Because of our son's inability to articulate his emotions appropriately and his sensory input remaining overloaded, he knew enough to make his best efforts to keep his emotions together while at public school. This meant that as soon as he was home in his "safe place," he erupted.

No name was too offensive, no aggression was out of bounds; we experienced a myriad of explosions every day from the time he woke up to the time he went to sleep. Things were thrown, insults were hurled—all in a painfully tearful attempt to tell us how he was feeling: out of control.

This became both my prison and my passion.

The judgment we felt daily from everyone from the school system to pediatricians, friends to fellow shoppers at our local grocery store, became paralyzingly isolating. In our rural Virginia town, there was no encouragement or support system for parents like us so we felt completely alone. And to make matters worse, I was an educator in the school system we were going to have to pull our son out of, so I was terrified.

So how does our son play into our mission to simplify our lives?

We were not living at all.

When You Feel Like You're Only Surviving

Friends, in that moment—in all of our moments during that season of parenting, surrounded by laundry and overcome by life—we were sincerely doing our absolute best to simply survive.

We were financially frustrated, emotionally spent, and completely overcome by what our 'dream' was looking like in reality for our little family. After researching, talking, and praying about it . . . a lot . . . we knew that simplifying our lives—specifically for us, living tiny—could be the solution to many of the obstacles that were keeping our family from thriving.

We simply refused to believe that God intended for us to just pay our bills and die. There had to be more. Joy had to be more than this mystical concept reserved for celebrities and biblical patriarchs.

When we made this intentional decision to simplify, our farmhouse sat on 15 acres in the county of our state with the highest unemployment rate, in the middle of the recession. Naturally, we assumed we'd have a long time for our dream to sit on the housing market. We knew we felt led to simplify, so listing our house was the first step and we could make plans while we went through that process.

Cue complete freak-out mode.

Our feelings to make the move to tiny living were validated when we listed our home that Sunday night at 11:09 p.m., and at 7:00 a.m. Monday morning, our realtor called to let us know there were three families in a bidding war over our house.

Y'all if you had a feather, you could've knocked me over with it and I'm a sizable girl!

So, in typical Burger family fashion, we decided we'd just go ahead and change everything in our lives . . . in about two weeks.

I accepted a job two states away teaching formerly incarcerated and at-risk youth and we had exactly 14 days to find a house, figure out a place to park, pack our stuff, tell our families (yikes), and move 600 miles away for a brand-new beginning where my husband would be a stay-at-home dad for the first time.

We knew we wanted to live tiny, but not even the greatest tiny house builders could have designed and constructed a tiny house in two weeks. So instead, we enlisted the help of a friend from high school who sold RVs.

We went on that Tuesday, purchased a used 36-foot, 2011 Jayco fifth wheel camper whose previous elderly owners were kind enough to leave the plastic on the carpet. We named her Telle (pronounced

Tell-lee). Tuesday night I called a little AirBnb host I found online in the county near my new teaching job, assured them that we weren't crazy, and asked if we could park our house on their property.

Friends, when I say that out loud, even now, I can't help but laugh. I was absolutely positive these folks would think we were serial killers and never call me again. But they called. That night. And they accepted.

So here we are, nearly two years later, still a little family of four, now living in 301 square feet instead of 2200. We were afraid to lose the privacy of our former 15-acres and we are now parked on a 20-acre farm, even bigger than what we had before, with a pond in our front yard, a shared garden space, and a stone's throw from bike paths connecting our entire state. The people we rent our land from have become like bonus grandparents to our kids. They are an absolute blessing.

Simplifying our lives has allowed us to become a one-income household where we are able to Roadschool our kiddos from wherever we're parked.

After writing for tiny house companies for a few months, I was invited to speak at a festival, which turned into more shows, which became nine speaking engagements in the first year.

In our first six months of simple living, we had almost paid off our debt, we were meeting our son's special needs, we were chasing dream careers, my diagnosed anxiety had decreased, our son's ability to succeed increased tenfold, and we were able to be intentional with every minute of our time.

Great, you might be saying, *but what about ME!?*

Can *I* Really Live Simply?

Maybe you have zero desire to live in a tiny house. Maybe you just picked this book up while you wait for your nail appointment and you are convinced, by now, that I am certifiably crazy. Or maybe you are just curious whether or not the life you had imagined could ever be your reality.

I am here to tell you it can be. This is coming from the mama who steadily ate a bag of chips while watching every episode of *The Biggest Loser,* convinced it could never be me.

But this *could* be your life.

You don't have to live in a tiny house or full-time RV
(although it is pretty much our best life)
to actually reclaim your joy.

Just ask yourself these questions:

Do you feel overwhelmed by work but know the mounting bills require you to log countless hours?

Do you feel trapped in a job that isn't your dream or utilizing your natural gifts?

Do you feel like you are missing out on the best parts of your family's lives because you are pulled in a million directions?

Are you strangled by anxiety or clutter or endless to-do lists?

Do you feel frustrated you are doing all that you can—but you never seem to get ahead?

Are you unhappy with your job/school/life?

Friends, if you said yes to any of these questions, **this book is for you.**

As we go through this journey, just remember we are in this *together.* I did it, too, and I will likely continue the process over and over because no one is never done growing or improving quality of life.

Throughout each chapter I will be giving you what I call, "The Rule of Five". These are five practical, easy to implement steps that apply to each phase we walk through.

Now, I can't promise you'll become *the prince of a town called Bel Air*, but I can assure you that you will laugh, you will reflect, and you will be given practical steps you can implement RIGHT NOW in your busy, overworked, exhausted season of life to help you start simplifying the chaos and start reclaiming joy!

Chapter 1
How to Let Go

"Downsizing can be hard, not just physically but emotionally, because you may have to give up things that have meaning for you. [I had] to keep reminding myself why I was doing it. In my case it was so my husband wouldn't have to commute anymore and we could be together every night."

-Leanne Stephens, Cooking In Small Spaces, Tiny Houses and Beyond

"Are you *sure* you don't want to keep it? I mean, look at it's googly eyes!" It was during our process of purging over 80% of our belongings to go tiny when I found myself in the floor of the playroom in our 2,200-square-foot farmhouse pleading with my then five-year-old son about why he actually *should* love the old school Fisher Price rotary phone my grandma had given him before she passed away.

Friends, he hadn't even ever seen a rotary phone in real life before.

It was in that moment I realized my son, barely more than a toddler, had a better grip on letting go than I did.

To my little boy, the toy was just a plastic box with big eyes and a pull string too small for anything taller than a baby to drag along, eyes blinking and faded colors flashing.

To me, that little vintage version of an old phone was a snapshot in time. It was the memory of his first birthday party when my grandma, having suffered a stroke but sometimes showing glimpses of her previously feisty and hysterical self, gifted that to our boy. It was the image in my mind of him on my parents' porch with his long, blonde curls blowing in the breeze as he leaned against her chest.

Shew, y'all! Even typing this turns me to a bundle of emotions—both happy and sad.

But in that moment on the playroom floor with my son, he taught me that no one could take the memories from me. The stuff was just that—*stuff.* Letting go of items was difficult because it somehow made me feel like I was giving up those remembrances of the people I loved; people who made me the woman and wife, mother and friend that I am now.

When It Isn't As Difficult

When we made the decision to downsize from 2,200 square feet to 300, we knew we would have to get rid of a lot of things, but no one can prepare you for just how much can be accumulated in over 12-years time. At that point in our relationship, my husband and I had lived in three houses, two basements, and a townhouse. We'd had two kids, and countless job changes.

Deciding to live in a home that only had room for what we'd actually use every day and enough clothes for one season at a time was a stressful relief.

Yes, we would have to go through all of the stuff we had packed away from all of our moves, but it gave us permission to rid ourselves of things we'd been holding onto for reasons even *we* didn't understand. And let me tell you how excited I was to unload the mountain of furniture collecting dust in our basement. It was like an antique store monument to every dead relative from either side of our family from the last two decades.

No matter the size of your home, simplifying your possessions can begin to give you clarity and allow space for you to breathe.

For years, we had both found it impossible to say no to family members wanting to pass things down to us, but what were we supposed to do with 42 antique wooden plant stands with marble table tops!? I mean, they were like spinning tops whose lids weighed 200 pounds and were just waiting to be pulled down on our small children's developing heads!

I am embarrassed to say there was also a room in our basement—in addition to the family's antique furniture warehouse—where suitcases and boxes lined the walls and storage shelves and, if my actual life depended on it, I couldn't have told you what was inside any of them. Those boxes had been packed no less than five years before—before having kids and grown-up jobs, before we were real life adults who paid mortgages and had enough rooms to store things no one wanted but everyone somehow deemed unnecessary to throw out themselves.

Who else has this room? Come on. I can't be the only one.

That room, in all of its dusty glory, went straight to the donation pile. I never even opened a box. I'm not crazy, but friends, if I hadn't needed it, looked for it, or used it in at least five years, I felt pretty confident in letting it go.

When You're Emotionally Attached

For some of us, letting go is generational. Maybe your family struggled financially so having much might mean freedom or a feeling of comfort. That can be a hard concept to overcome.

Maybe your family has always been sentimental so giving away something meaningful feels wrong. Perhaps you just can't get over the memories associated with some of your things, even if they are your great grandfather's uncle's third cousin's cello that would clearly never fit in a tiny house or in anyone's version of simplified living (unless, of course, you play the cello).

It's okay, guys. We are in this together. First, we breathe.

And now, we get to work.

Five Steps to Begin to Cut The Cord

1. Go Through Each Room

If you are anything like me—and I have to assume you are, at least a little—you have "memories" (read: stuff that reminds you of people enough that you don't want to part with it) tucked away in every corner of every room in your house. You might have toys in the kids' playroom, blankets and quilts in the living room, paintings stashed under the basement stairs, and knick-knacks scattered everywhere else.

In this first step, you need to go through each room in your home and look for anything you'd feel uncomfortable giving away or selling because of a memory or person it is tied to in your mind. Take those items and box them up. (Don't freak out, Karen. You don't have to get rid of them yet. We are only in step one.)

2. Pick A Storage Spot

Once you've boxed items, choose a room in your home you don't frequent; think about that guest bedroom that goes unvisited or the basement storage area. This is where your boxes of memories will live for the next 30 days—one month. You can do it.

If you don't have an extra room in your house, ask a friend to use a closet or pay the $50 for a storage unit for the sake of the process. Trust me. You need to have everything somewhere you cannot and will not easily access it.

Now, leave it alone for 30 days. Breathe, Karen. You can do this!

3. Cut It In Half

You made it! Thirty days in, you may now revisit your memories. You're welcome.

Unbox every single item. Spread them out in front of you on a bed or the floor so you can see every one. As you look at the different things that have made such an impression on you over the years, start the downsizing process.

Which items did you genuinely miss seeing this month? Are there things you or your family members actually use that you'd put in those boxes?

When my grandma passed I actually didn't want things like jewelry because, to me, that wasn't *her.* I kept her potato masher. I had other little trinkets and things, too, but those eventually didn't make the cut. However, that potato masher is still in my kitchen being given life by my little family.

As you are filtering through your piles, count your total items. The goal for this step is to cut them in half. That means if you had packed away 40 items, you are only allowed to take 20 into the next step. You can donate what didn't make the cut, or you can even gift items to others in your family so they can get new life, but they can't come with you.

4. Out of Sight, Out of Mind

Don't you feel better—lighter somehow? See, I told you we could do this!

Now that you have done an excellent job of decreasing items that are difficult for you to let go, box them back up. They probably liked the quiet of their little box anyway.

This month, place a note somewhere you'll see each day, like the fridge or your bathroom mirror. List items you've thought about during their second 30 days of storage. They may only make the list if you organically think of them **more than twice** during the month.

5. Cut It In Half Again

Calm down, Karen, this is for your own good. Take your list of the items you thought about more than once and pull them from the boxes. Then, if it feels necessary, unpack everything and simply cut the remaining number in half again.

It was much easier for me, after that first 60 days had passed, to let go of things I was consciously not using but previously felt compelled to hold onto. I realized by then that I still had every single memory but I didn't have to deal with the "stuff" that came along with them.

There you have it! I knew you could do it!

Friends, I know this process can be emotional. It may be that you've lost loved ones whose impact runs so deep in your bones you can sometimes still smell them. I get it, I do. But stick with me.

I promise you the people I am thinking of when I describe that feeling of missing someone I loved, I am certain they'd want me to be living the life I am living now; not the life of paycheck-to-paycheck or the life where I am so tired and stressed I can barely function, and definitely not the life where I have to work so many hours to pay for "stuff" that my family doesn't get the best of me.

No one can take the memories and only *you* can choose the freedom that comes from giving away the "stuff".

A Note on Photos

Depending on your age, you are either thinking, "Thank you Lord! I was afraid she was going to tell me to start with my old Polaroids and begin tossing out my albums!" Or, if you are on the other end on the age spectrum, you might be saying something like, "Wait a second, why are photos important? I already have them saved on my phone, the Cloud, Instagram, Twitter, Facebook, Snapchat, and so on ..."

If you are of my generation or older, (I am 36 as I write this), you understand the tie to photographs just as much as you remember loving the smell of books with real pages and having to look things up in a card catalog instead of a computer because those were basically only for avoiding dying of dysentery while playing Oregon Trail.

For those of us who grew up in the Olan Mills, JCPenney Portrait Studios, Glamour Shot days, we—and our parents—likely have piles and albums of baby photos of us propped up all willy nilly as newborn babies on a piece of grass turf. There are family shots where our siblings look as if they are appearing from the darkness by some sort of magical force in the upper right hand corner while the rest of us are minding our own business, looking off into the distance like normal people.

Friends, these and the photos that are black and white and boast stellar images of our grandparents as children who were apparently not ever allowed to smile, and the Victorian looking ones whose eyes seem to follow you as you move can be—hear me when I say—thrown away.

GASP! "No she didn't!" Oh yes, yes I did, Karen. And this one is totally reasonable so hang with me here.

Unless you are genuinely interested in your family lineage or the history that comes with decorating your home with these pictures, you can take one of a few routes to memorialize your images digitally so they aren't taking up space and making your house smell like someone's grandma's basement.

Options for Photo Storage

1. Make a scrapbook

2. Convert to a video

3. Have them copied onto a disc

4. Copy them to a USB drive

5. Save them to the Cloud

*If you are unsure what some of these options entail or how to go about them, allow me to recommend the world wide web because this is a book about simplicity and not computers. I still secretly wonder what "the Cloud" even is and where in the heck my documents actually go when I store them there!

Shew. Okay, Karen. Can we still be friends? Yes, I told you to get rid of the boxes and boxes of old family photos, but think of the memories you'll have as you go through them! We now have options for storing them more appropriately and in ways that will last much longer than in their originally printed format.

*Note: If your name is actually Karen, I want to meet you because I have a lot to talk about. I have no reason why, but I always refer to this fictional person who judges me and my lifestyle/parenting/ability to properly adult, and I imagine her name is Karen and she likely works in Human Resources. So my apologies to any real-life Karens reading this and feeling personally attacked. I am sure you are super sweet and thoughtful. I owe you a coffee.

Chapter 2
Start Small

"Simplicity is a bit of a misnomer. There is nothing simple about it. It goes against everything we've been taught, the American dream. It tells us that bigger isn't better. It tells us that better makes us bigger."

-Andrew Odom

"The more I let go of, the happier I was. The less stuff in our house, the more freely I could breathe."

-Shawna Nyquist, Presence Over Perfect

Once you have tackled the emotional traumas that can ebb and flow when downsizing your stuff so you can simplify your life, the rest is easy. As we go through this process, step-by-step together, letting go of things, reducing your usage of "stuff", and decluttering your everyday will start to feel so natural and so rewarding that you will hardly remember when it felt difficult in the beginning.

Throughout our journey here, you will have the opportunity to hear some tips from people actually living this lifestyle. One of our family's favorite things about having downsized and gone tiny is the incredible community of like-minded folks who really rally around one another in this idea of simplified living and reclaiming the joy that life has for us.

Carmen Shenk, author of *Kitchen Simplicity* and known in the tiny home industry as The Tiny House Foodie, recommends that we not forget the "S.O.A.P."

> **S**tart small—but start
>
> **O**nly one right-sizing project at a time
>
> **A**ppreciate the process and stay in the moment
>
> **P**ractice gratitude

Let's break it down.

Like this chapter suggests, we are going to start small, but start nonetheless. We are only going to tackle one right-sizing project at a time. Notice here that she uses the phrase "right-sizing"—not "downsizing" or even "tiny"—because the size that seems right for you and your needs will become obvious as you go through the process and it doesn't have to look like what feels right to me or anyone else.

Next, Carmen recommends that, "We appreciate the process and stay in the moment." Trusting this process will be challenging at times because we are conditioned, having lived in a consumer-driven society, that more is more. This entire idea of simplifying goes against what we've known or seen as success, achievement, and the American dream. So stick with me.

"Practice gratitude" is my favorite of Carmen's action steps because this is one we often miss but it is, perhaps, the most powerful. When we choose to live with less, it allows us to walk in gratitude for the things that made the cut—the items, clothing, shoes, accessories, toys, furniture, artwork, hobby materials, books, and photos we intentionally chose to keep in our lives. Each of these items brings us happiness or it wouldn't have made it this far in your process. Be thankful.

As we begin this process of simplification together, be encouraged knowing that you've already tackled the emotional stuff. Now we take it one room at a time . . . and sometimes, just one drawer or cabinet at a time. This should be freeing and even fun, not stressful or overwhelming.

"Don't try to go through your closet all at one time. Go through it in three separate sweeps. First, go through and pull out all the damaged (or stained) items. Then, go back through a second time and get rid of everything that's too young, old, small or large for you. Then, when all you have left are "viable" options . . . go through one last time and get rid of anything that you haven't worn in the last year." - Jenn Baxter, former tiny house owner

So as we move forward, we will take the simplification process one step at a time, one room at a time. We'll keep our focus on enjoying how we feel as we rid our home, our space, and ourselves of so much "stuff", so much clutter, and so much weight that we've carried around, stacked and stored away for years.

For you notetakers like myself, here is a summary of your **Rule of Five:**

1. Start small—but start

2. Only one right-sizing project at a time

3. Appreciate the process and stay in the moment

4. Practice gratitude

5. **Break it Down-**Like we tell our son, "You can see the big picture or the end goal, but don't let it freak you out. Every destination starts with the first step."

This is going to feel so freeing and so life-changing that no matter your end goals—living simply, relieving anxiety, creating more time to enjoy your family, reclaiming joy—you will be so glad you committed to the process. Your only regret will be that you didn't do it sooner!

Chapter 3
Kitchen Clean Up

"Suddenly I was in this tiny kitchen learning to cook a completely different way. I realized I was making food the old-school way. Great food, simply prepared."

-Carmen Shenk, Kitchen Simplicity

I distinctly remember purging my kitchen.

Over the years, we had collected an embarrassing amount of ridiculous small appliances—blenders that only mixed one thing, like cookie batter or smoothies, but never both. We had an onion chopper, an electric coffee grinder (though I have exactly zero memories of ever buying whole bean coffee), and a knife sharpener but no less than three sets of cheap kitchen knives, so you would assume at least one knife would always remain sharp.

Maybe it was growing up in a powerful matriarchal family, or perhaps it was the distinct memory of the smell of simmering chicken stock and the feel of the flour on my eight-year-old hands as my grandma let us help roll out dough for homemade noodles, but the kitchen was difficult for me to purge.

Of course, like any good Midwestern girl who is also a little bit sassy, I loved my brightly-colored Fiestaware dishes, but those weren't why my kitchen was hard to simplify and put in a box. Friends, my kitchen was *full* of silver gravy ladles, oversized mixing bowls, wooden dough rollers, and an electric knife we only used on Thanksgiving and Easter. They didn't begin their lives in my home, but in the houses of my aunt and my grandma. Those dishes had made countless meals to be set on the oval-shaped table where my entire family gathered to eat and laugh and play cards on Sundays after church.

We start purging, decluttering, and organizing in the kitchen because that is a room in most homes where people tend to spend at least some amount of time during each day.

When you're hosting guests, it's also a place where people tend to gather. We want it to feel inviting, but we also want to create a space you are proud of and where people *want* to spend their time. We want you to *want* to make your memories here.

But let's remember our basics: we start small.

This is another great reason to begin in the kitchen since there are so many opportunities for small tasks to tackle so you can gain momentum and confidence as you work through simplifying your life.

Here are your **Five Steps to a Simple, Healthy Kitchen**. Follow them—in order. You promised, remember Karen? Trust the process and remember we are in this together.

1. Start in the Pantry

Whether you are doing your first or your 50th purge, always start in the pantry. This is one of the smallest and most manageable places in any room of any home where you can throw out the old and organize the new without too much emotion or feelings of overwhelm.

Start by throwing out anything with old dates; sort like items together in piles on a counter; then reorganize when you put away, placing the same items in order with the earliest expiration dates in front.

We use can organizers in our pantry cupboard and a magnetic spice rack on our freezer to get the most efficient use out of our vertical space since we live tiny. These same space-saving methods can be applied in a bathroom or home office or any room regardless of the size of your home.

2. Counters Are Not For Storage

This step tends to hurt people's feelings. Look, Karen, step away from your hoardie stack of junk mail and old receipts. You are never going to need to find your second grader's proofs from kindergarten picture day ever again. Just throw it out!

Invest in a few organizing hacks like a solid mail organizer that doubles as your key holder and a place to store the dog's leash. This will only hold a certain amount of mail so it forces you to throw out nonessentials.

I also recommend storing small items like medications in a bin (if you don't have small children around), coffee-making supplies, or grab-and-go snacks like granola bars . This keeps things in their place and encourages those of us who may tend to naturally collect a junk pile to put things where they belong—and leave the counter space free for food prep or gathering around as a family.

3. Move to the Drawers

If you have a junk drawer do just that—junk it! How many of us, for some reason beyond human explanation, have kept old D batteries, a tube of chapstick from 1989, 30 paperclips that are tangled together, a gross green penny, and a pocket knife from Scouts just laying in a drawer somewhere in your kitchen between the old telephone book no one has used this decade and a dish towel with Santa embroidered on the front?

Guilty!

Once that is tackled, the rest should be a breeze! There are only seven days in a week so there is absolutely no explainable reason to have more than that number of dish towels or wash cloths, sponges or cleaning supplies in your drawers. Same with silverware.

In our home, we have four of everything. There are four of us so we have four forks, four knives, four spoons, and four kid sets of silverware since our youngest is still learning. We also have two paring knives, two steak knives, a cheese knife, a bread knife, a butcher knife, and kitchen shears. The end. That is it.

We have one drawer for our kitchen utensils that we still go through when we continue to purge, because if we haven't used it, we have to get rid of it. Since counters are not for storage, these are in a drawer instead of one of those spinning racks we used to have collecting dust on our kitchen counter.

This drawer has an ice cream scoop, a pizza cutter, an apple corer, two cutting boards (one for meat), a whisk, a set of three bamboo spoons, a slotted spoon, a spaghetti spoon, a can strainer, a vegetable peeler, an orange slicer, a zucchini noodle maker, and, of course, my grandma's potato masher.

Go through your drawers. What do you *need*? What are you actually using each month? Each day?

Give it one week and everything you actually use, store on one counter (Cool it, Karen. I know what I said in number two. This is just an experiment!).

Once your week is up, take note and begin to pack up and give away the things just taking up space.

4. Appliances are Next—Large and Small

We get this tip from one of my great friends in the tiny house industry, Jenn Baxter.

She had her 160-square-foot tiny house on wheels built and featured on HGTV.

Jenn tells us to, "Get rid of all those 'one hit wonders' that are taking up space in your kitchen cabinets, which are all of those cute, trendy appliances that serve one very specific (and usually rare) purpose. Things like cotton candy machines, cake pop makers and sandwich irons. If you don't use them at least once or twice a week, they need to go!"

Remember the cookie batter only mixer and the smoothie only maker? They had to go for us. And, unless you live off of smoothies, they need to go for you too.

If your family never uses your microwave, or uses your stove burners but not the oven, make adjustments in your appliances. This can save you not only on the upfront costs, but on maintenance and utilities if you opt for a cooktop only or apartment-sized over standard appliance.

5. Dishes First—and Glasses and Mugs and Plates and . . .

Same concept applies as before. Pay close attention to what you use. If you are a coffee drinker, like I am, you might keep a couple extra mugs around than you would wine glasses or drinking cups.

This process is becoming easier, right? You are basically a professional now! Keep it up because we have a few more rooms to go; you will really start to feel like you have less responsibility, less to clean (one of my favorite parts), and you will love the feeling of blessing others with things you had just been storing for years.

Chapter 4
Leave Space for Magic in the Bedroom

"Life is a balance of holding on and letting go."

-Author Unknown

"This is a chance to design a space around everything you need...and nothing you don't."

-Johanna Elsner, Perch & Nest Tiny Homes

"Live simply so that others may simply live."

-Gandhi

The bedroom is where things tend to get personal for people. This isn't about forcing you to part with the scarf your favorite grandmother gave you before she passed away. If you love the scarf and wear the scarf, honey, scarf it up! This lesson is more about prying your fingers from the box of baseball cards you haven't opened since fourth grade, or getting rid of the totes full of pre-pregnancy clothes that, if we are being really honest, we aren't likely to ever wear again.

Making room for the magic that can happen in your bedroom when it is free of clutter, old (unwanted) memories, and piles of things you won't ever use, need, or wear again frees up space for you to move, to dance, to read, to work, or to just enjoy the peace that comes with empty space.

So here are your **Five Steps to Keeping the Bedroom Magical.**

1. Make Cuts In Your Closet

I will honestly never forget the first purge of our closet. In our giant farmhouse, we had our first and only walk-in closet. It felt ginormous. I mean, I felt like a celebrity should be getting dressed in there. My side of the walk-in had never been full in the entire four years we lived there.

I am not much of a person for style and if you saw me in my three-day yoga pants and hoodie, you'd be able to tell that for yourself.

My husband, on the other hand, is what we like to affectionately call a "div-o". It's like a diva for men. He is a hard-working man's man, but when it comes to an opportunity to go out, sister, his boots match his sunglasses which accent his outfit, which are capped off by a hat that brings the whole ensemble together.

If you need me, I'll be over here not knowing how to dress myself.

So, when we first went through our closet to purge, I spent a lot of time laughing while my husband was in a lot of denial.

When you go through your initial closet purge, don't focus on counting your number of items. Simply do a once-over of your closet, shoes, accessories, and any dresser drawers. If you haven't worn it since high school, friend, put it in the pile to donate or throw away. Trust me, your old cheer uniform that wouldn't fit if your life depended on it might make a little girl at the thrift shop very excited, but it has no business collecting dust at your house.

2. Reduce Your Decor

If you rock a bachelor pad look of bare bedroom walls and a single rug, this step may be an easy one. For those like me, who can't step away from a good Pinterest-inspired photo collage, this one might be a tad painful.

During this step, your goal is to streamline the decor in your bedroom. If you love books, but you keep a dusty stack by your nightstand you haven't opened in months (because...kids), then donate them and see about renting audio versions to listen to on your commute to work.

If you have wall decor, cut it in half. If you are happily single, married, or otherwise interested in sex, do yourself a favor and attempt to rid your intimate space of pictures of your kids. I'm heartless, I know Karen. But it can honestly make a difference if you don't have family members or little infant eyes peering at you during those otherwise private moments.

Additionally, as we said in the kitchen, counters are not for clutter. This includes your nightstand or bedside table. If you don't have one, invest in a small table with a drawer to put your unmentionables so the tabletop doesn't need to house more than an alarm clock, a lamp, and maybe a single book or framed picture. If you are one who sets your alarm on your phone (ahem, guilty!) try docking it at a charging station in an office or desk space to encourage you to step away from the screen to improve your sleep habits and provide opportunity for more uninterrupted magical bedroom time. You can thank me later.

3. The Hanger Test

Set a time frame to accomplish this one. I took a month, but you may only need a week or two. Others (eh-hem, my husband) may want to plan for longer.

For the hanger test, you want to clear a space in your hanging closet as well as one single drawer in your dresser. This is your usable space.

For the next period of time you've designated, you need to place every item of clothing that you've actually worn (once you've washed it, of course) in the designated area. Over the course of your weeks to month, you will get a clear visual of how many items of clothes, shoes, and accessories you've actually worn.

47

Friends, it is *shocking* how much space we waste housing things we sincerely never, ever wear or use.

Once the time you've determined comes to an end, take a look at what is currently residing in your hanger and drawer space.

How many pairs of shoes did you actually wear?

How many pairs of jeans were left untouched?

How many accessories are still sitting still in a jewelry box or on a shelf?

This may take some soul-searching, but that visual will help you with step five in this process.

As an additional measure, you can place a brightly-colored yard sale sticker on the stem of each hanger that remained used during that time. You may have found that you have 112 items hanging in your closet but only 21 (or even 6) of the hanging items were actually worn. Sticker those hangers and give it another two weeks. See if you can stick to those items alone or were more added into the rotation?

4. Two Sets of The Necessities

It is important to note that all underthings—think panties/underwear, socks, bras, sports bras, hosiery—are considered necessities so they are not to be counted in step five. You can keep as many of those as you think you need. Once this simplification starts to take hold, I am confident you will part ways with some of them naturally.

In this step, necessities in the bedroom are things like pillows, sheet sets, comforters, or quilts. Think of the things you might need to wash in the bedroom and want an extra set of while things are being laundered. If you have a master bathroom, this would also include bath towels.

It happens often that families find themselves with an entire spare closet or drawer overflowing with random sheets, pillow cases, and the like—many of which they never use or forget existed. This is the time when you find someone who could use those extras or donate them.

5. The Closet's Final Cut: 50 Items Per Person, Per Season

As mentioned in step four, this rule of thumb does not apply to your underthings, only shoes, clothes, outerwear, and accessories.

This step may push you, but if you've stayed on track this far, you can do this.

Just before going tiny, our family instituted the rule of 50 items per person, per season. Since we stay primarily parked in locations that have four seasons, it is important that we have an off-season bin stored away with clothes we aren't currently wearing. This does *not* mean we have four different wardrobes. We have two; one for cool/cold weather, and one for warm/hot weather.

Go back through your used hanger and drawer items and count them. If you were to only keep those items for the current season, how many would you still need to get rid of, or would you have space to add a few more things to the mix?

If you live in a climate that is primarily one season year-round, you might consider increasing your number of items since you wouldn't need to completely change out your clothes during the year.

A caution to parents: I would keep a tote of clothing and shoes the next size up, as children tend to hit growth spurts unexpectedly and you don't want to find yourself stuck.

My favorite part of this final step is that it allows you to get down to the nitty gritty of your wardrobe. Friends, I had two—as in more than one—totes FULL of clothes I hadn't worn since college. No amount of post-baby body would ever make it back into those outfits and giving them away felt incredible.

No longer did I feel those totes staring at me with their judgy size 8/10 eyes. Now, I was able to give my good quality clothing to friends who could actually use and wear them right now. They got use out of things that had been collecting dust for years waiting for me to magically lose 50 pounds.

Every day since this particular step of our purge, I have been able to enjoy the freedom to get dressed and *know* I will feel confident in what I put on. I didn't keep anything I didn't feel good about. With our ongoing purges, if I haven't worn it since the previous purge, it has to go.

Somewhere along the path, it becomes less about fear and more about freedom.

Now that you've made it through the bedroom purge, you can enjoy the spoils of your labor. You have, no doubt, increased the empty and clean space in your room. You have surely blessed others with your donated goods. And you are now ready to enter the next phase with a solid wardrobe you use and love.

Chapter 5
Clutter from Kids

"We chose the simple life for our family. We want to raise a generation of mindful, conscious humans who choose experiences over possessions."

-Emily Gerde, Minimalist Living For a Maximum Life

"Children need time to become themselves— through play and social interaction. If you overwhelm a child with stuff—with choices and pseudo-choices—before they are ready, they will only know one emotional gesture: More!"

-Kim John Payne, Simplicity Parenting: Using the Extraordinary Power of Less to Raise Calmer, Happier, and More Secure Kids

About once or twice a month, I have the incredible opportunity to talk to crowds gathered for a common goal that is either centered on simple living or on bettering education for kids, specifically for, as I call them, extreme children. This is my passion and it is one I am grateful to have the opportunity to pursue.

When I use my platform to speak to those audiences or a friend at a coffee shop, or even Karen in the grocery line, I always try to let them know how brilliant kids are. I am not the helicopter parent who lives vicariously through a child I deem next to perfection. I am talking about *all* children.

See, kids are born into the world wanting only one thing—*one*—love.

They don't cry for toys. They don't throw fits for vacations. And they aren't sad because they don't have new phones . . . not until they are *taught* these behaviors. Our jobs as parents intentionally choosing a life of simplicity is to love our children—to fiercely advocate for them while simultaneously allowing them to be their own best selves. If that means we let them fail, mess up, even fall and scrape their knees, those are the lessons that will stick with them and those are opportunities for them to develop crucial life skills.

Cool it, Karen. I am not suggesting we volunteer our wee ones for danger. I am just saying if we, as the wise adults we think we are, would sit back and listen to our kids play, watch them observe a situation, and see what they choose to emulate or gravitate toward, we might learn something.

Remember the scene from the playroom floor in our farmhouse? Had I not taken a cue from my son that the memories weren't in the "stuff", I might have missed out and drug around boxes full of memories I already had without the extra baggage.

So get ready to work, friends, because here are our **Five Rules for Purging with Kids.**

1. The Rule of THEIRS

As you prepare to purge in your kids' rooms, playroom, and all of the baskets, boxes, and cute little cubby-like shelves your kids have claimed throughout your house, you need to begin to wrap your mind around *The Rule of Theirs*.

This was not an easy one for me to accept, being that I am exceptionally Type A and like things done my way or . . . well, also still done my way.

This rule is simple: If a toy, book, or otherwise recreational item was bought by them or given to them as a gift—even from you—it is theirs to determine whether it stays or goes. That means they get to pick. Period.

No nagging, bribing, or incredibly unconvincing uses of reverse psychology. If they want to keep it, it stays; if not, it goes.

2. Tackle the Toys

For the average American home, a child receives 70 new toys each year—SEVENTY. I mean, unless we are talking Micro Machines of the early 90s variety, that is a lot of space, a lot of storage, and a *lot* of toys that are likely spending the majority of their shelf lives not being played with.

For this step, you have your child (you may need to assist, depending on his or her age—but remember the Rule of Theirs) spread out each like toy item and count them. My son always starts with his superheroes. Once they are counted, you direct your child to cut these items in half.

Just breathe, Karen. I am not asking you to Goodwill $1,000 worth of last year's Beanie Babies.

From here, the adult has a decision to make: donate, yard sale, social media sell, or library system these items. We gave away countless toys in our purges getting to 300 square feet, but now we use a tote.

Our children get two of those fabric bins I told you about earlier and their toys have to fit in them or they must go. Anything we don't give away, or toys they seldom play with, we store in a large plastic tote at a family member's house. Every few weeks, our kids take a bag of toys from our home and exchange them with a few items from that tote.

This makes our kids excited because it feels like they get brand new toys, it uses what would've otherwise been sitting at the bottom of a toy box, and it costs us zero dollars.

Library system. Everybody wins.

3. Focus on Clothes

Our house follows two simple rules when it comes to clothing: *New In, Old Out*, and *50 Items Per Person, Per Season*.

This means we purged our kids' clothing . . .a *lot* of it. We had holiday outfits and old costumes, shoes they'd never worn because they skipped sizes and no less than six entire tubs of clothes from when our oldest was born and we just weren't convinced we were done having kids.

It all found new homes where people actually needed it—right then and not in an imaginary five years *if* we had another child.

Choose clothing that is the size they wear right now. Choose only the season it is currently. Be sure to include shoes in your 50 items (but not underclothes like socks and underwear).

In addition to what they are wearing right now, remember the off-season, next size bin in our storage compartment. That holds any clothes for the upcoming season, hand-me-downs we might receive from friends and family for the next size up, or anything I might find a deal on but they cannot fit into yet. This allows me to be prepared as seasons change and kids grow without committing to an entire closet full of stuff they'll never wear more than once.

4. Re-tackle the Toys

It is worth saying that this is the time we lay the toys out again, each with their like items, count them, and cut them in half again.

Unless you already have this minimalism thing down, your kids have likely tricked you into the Target dollar bin items or some crane machine stuffed animal they never even sleep with since your first round. So this is when they go bye-bye!

5. Reduce the Books

Full disclosure: this one hurts my feelings.

Maybe this is just the English teacher in me, but I have always loved books. In fact, parting with my own library when we downsized was one of my hardest places to reduce. Our kids had eleventy billion books before we went tiny.

To focus your purge, choose one shelf where books will live. For us, this is a shared shelf near our kids' beds with a separate bookshelf for their Roadschool items, since those books are different and they rotate in and out with lessons.

Like each of the previous steps, we lay them out and cut them in half. Unless there are a few favorites your child reads over and over, allow them to be quick to dismiss some books they've already read and pass those on to a new home. Many towns now have little free libraries built in local parks where you can donate (and borrow) books.

For the future, we stick to consignment bookstores, online homeschool resale shops, and, of course, the library. This is a grossly underused resource in most communities.

Allow your kids to teach you along the way, and remember that reducing their overstimulation and access to instant gratification and an overwhelming amount of choices every day, every hour, every minute is actually helping them to hone in, focus, and be kind.

Chapter 6
Intentional Gift-Giving

"For as long as we've practiced simplicity as a family we have constantly had to remind ourselves that it isn't about getting a smile from someone. It's about giving as many smiles as we can."

- Andrew Odom

Though Christmas isn't the only time we give gifts throughout the year, it tends to be the spotlighted holiday for such things. For that reason, we'll use it as our illustration for this step.

Christmas in a tiny house looks the same for our little family as it did when we lived in a sprawling 2,200-square-foot farmhouse. The only differences are that our tree is tall and skinny, our stockings are smaller (as if the original ones shrank in the dryer), and we are honestly *much* happier.

As much as Americans complain that Christmas shouldn't be about gifts and going into debt and holiday stress, for many, it is. For our family, it has looked eerily similar in the past. However, since going tiny in August of 2017, our family puts even less emphasis on "stuff" than we did before. So the pressure to outdo everyone else's Pinterest-perfect holiday is relieved because we choose to focus on simplicity.

Our kids are currently seven and almost three-years-old and we have an Elf on the Shelf, we go tour Christmas lights, we visit Santa and do the whole thing. However, our children always know the expectation. Our family celebrates Christmas with *giving* in mind.

So here are your **Five Rules for Intentional Gift-Giving**.

1. Serve Others First

In our home, we emphasize two simple rules: 1. In everything, be kind, and 2. Always be respectful. To model this for our kids, we make sure they are keeping those virtues at the forefront, especially during times of year that could otherwise be consumed with greed. Focusing on simplicity is a great way to start shedding old habits of spending too much and collecting "stuff".

Our Elf brings the kids kindness tasks and challenges them to come up with ideas of their own. We also do a family service project during the month of December to keep service at the center of our celebration. I know other moms who do this on birthdays, as well.

Cool it, Karen. It doesn't mean we don't throw birthday parties or buy gifts, it just means we are servant-minded first.

Don't be concerned if you've never done it before. There are so many wonderful ways to bless others and none of them have to be over the top. The greatest part is seeing how excited your kids get when they begin to understand how wonderful it is to bless other people with simple acts of kindness. This time you spend serving together becomes a gift in itself, and it can cost nothing.

Service Opportunity Ideas:

- Local Food Bank
- Local Soup Kitchen

- Make Cards for your V.A. hospital

- Go Caroling at a Nursing Home

- Deliver a Meal to Teachers

- Make Holiday Baskets for the Salvation Army

- Give $5 Gift Cards at a Counseling Center

- Make Care Packages for Homeless Shelters

- Learn to Crochet and Make Scarves and Hats for Homeless Shelters

2. DIY Gifts

My husband and I have always worked in either social work or education so our paychecks have never been anything to write home about. For that reason, since our very first Christmas together we've hand-made gifts. Some have been hysterical and others tearfully thoughtful and sweet. The goal is to spend as little money as possible and create something you think the other person will enjoy.

It doesn't matter if you earn a large salary or have an impressive savings. This can still be an incredible way to make a big impact with a small gesture.

Since having kids, we've passed the tradition down to them. We still buy some gifts as well, but this one task allows us to set aside time to specifically think about what someone else in the family would love that we can make ourselves.

This step toward simplicity also allows you to eliminate buying frivolous "things" that are not likely to make it through your next house purge anyway. Instead, you spend your money on things your gift recipient really wants or really needs.

3. Gift Experiences Over Things

This is an idea that is finally catching on. Parents have always joked that you can give a kid the most expensive toy and he will instead play with the box.

That is a perfect example of why experiences far exceed any toy or tangible gift.

Kids don't care about the latest and greatest toys or gadgets nearly as much as they do about spending quality time with the people who love them most. The same can be said of people at any age. Gifting experiences provides moments to make magic ourselves and create memories together. For our kids, who tend to have above-average energy levels, it also makes for safe space to run, jump, climb, and shriek with excitement, minus the penalty for acting like the mayor of Crazy Town.

Children's Experience Gift Ideas:

- Local Zoo Membership

- Local Museum Membership

- Subscription Boxes

- Trampoline Park

- Fondue Restaurant

- Cooking Lessons

4. Choose Gifts That Do Double Duty

If there is something your birthday boy really wants or needs this year, give gifts that are both meaningful and practical. With simplicity in mind, it is always better to purchase quality items over quantity. They may cost a little more in the beginning, but they will last the recipient much longer, producing less clutter and waste.

If you can find something with more than one purpose, that is a great gift with simplicity at its center. If someone needs a desk, buy her one that is wall-mounted and folds down so it can also be a place that houses office supplies while tucking away to save space. If she is looking for a kitchen item, try to find one with other uses built in, such as a cork screw that doubles as a clever wine topper or bottle opener.

5. Provide an Opportunity to Start Pursuing a Dream

No matter the ages of the people you are shopping for, consider something they are passionate about. What is something that gives them great joy or that people constantly tell them they are good at doing? Those are the dreams that have yet to be realized for most of us, so why not create an opportunity with an intentional gift that provides them the space to use their talents to pursue something they love?

Opportunity Gift Ideas:

- Music/Singing Lessons

- Dance Class

- Space Camp

- Art Courses

- Sip and Paint date

- Writing Course

- Construction Site tour

- Police Ride-Along

- Race Car Driving experience

Even before going tiny, we were a pretty minimalist family existing in a world where we just couldn't keep up. Simple living brought everything into perspective and allowed us to create a life that fit our needs and left little room for wants that weren't necessary. Teaching this idea to our kids has been an amazing learning opportunity for all of us.

During Christmas, or any time you give gifts, challenge yourselves to focus on others, create something with your own hands, and give the gift of time. Those simple suggestions can truly make it a season of simplicity and meaningful giving at any age.

Chapter 7
Former Must-Haves We Decided to Ditch

"You can lose it all—all the things you thought mattered most—and rise up to tell a different story."

-Jen Hatmaker, *Interrupted*

It is pretty incredible, as you begin to downsize and purge yourself of non-necessities, what you find you no longer need or haven't used in years. Like us, many people uncover entire boxes they hadn't ever even unpacked. It is likely that you have an attic or basement stockpile as well. Most people do.

So here are your **Five Rules for Former Must-Haves You Might Decide to Ditch.**

1. Multiple Seasons/Sizes of Clothing

Full transparency, if left to their own devices, most moms can become hoarders.

Whether we grew up with limited funds teaching us to be thrifty and responsible, or we are just preparing for future sizes for our kids, we can end up with totes and closets filled with stuff. This preparedness includes couponing for groceries, buying in bulk, and snagging deals on clothes or shoes before our kids can even fit into the sizes.

Whether you are focused on simplicity for the sake of organization or you are aiming to downsize your living space, stored items should drastically decrease. This means, aside from maybe a dresser and closet space, it is good to aim for one tote or drawer for the next season's items. So, when changing over your wardrobe from winter to spring, everything that can still be worn next winter must fit into the drawer.

Simplistic living can be viewed in totes, if you haven't already caught on.

This mindset has cut down on excessive spending as well as offered us a true picture of what we actually wear.

So, if it doesn't fit in the tote you've deemed as "off-season" or "next-size up" for your kids, it has to go. Sorry, Karen. No room in the inn.

2. Extras of Everything

It shocks many to discover their kids don't need 20 pair of any one thing and the dog can still be happy if she runs out of dog treats.

As a former bulk for budget shopper, simple living forced me to re-think my entire grocery buying process. I might have previously had 9 bags of dog treats or an entire shelf filled with toilet paper just because it was on sale. However, all of those things just took up space and I have never had anyone report finding themselves in a state of dog treat-less panic.

So, fellow saving-savvy friends, step away from the fast food sauce packets. It's fine. You have a bottle of BBQ sauce in your fridge. You will make it through this nugget crisis without taking 13 extra packets home with you, Karen. Trust me.

3. Trendy Toys and Gadgets

Most people focused on simplicity find themselves encouraged to spend more time outdoors since the interior clutter is decreased and things feel more open. Because of that, neither they nor their kiddos find the need to spend the scientific American average of eleventy billion hours on a screen or cell phone.

Most operate on the rule that if they get something new, something old is replaced. Like us, many still purge toys about once every 6-8 weeks so the kids know to expect it. This can be very freeing because they can simply employ a toy library system like we mentioned in step two of chapter six.

Digital items are no exception. Each person shouldn't need more than one in the home at any given time. Remember, the focus of living simply is to spend our time together and on growth and fulfillment of dream chasing over "stuff" and mindless time wasting.

I know, Karen, it seems like child abuse to take your child's iPad, but I promise we lived through the computer-less 80s and so will he. And you both will thank me for it later when you've spent time together—like real, quality time in conversation or play. It's pretty epic when families figure out how to bond again over simple things like blanket forts or movie nights.

I am not suggesting that your kids never work on a laptop, own a cell phone, or play games on an iPad, but I am saying limiting them to one item per member of the household will help to refocus the family on quality time.

4. "Just In Case" Items

Natural disasters occur but they are rare. This means it is unlikely you will need to make the space for a 'Go Bag' or the 30 pieces of fine china most people keep in a specially designated cabinet in case the Queen comes over. You don't need these things so rid yourself of them. Experience the freeing power of only keeping what you are certain you will use.

And can we please talk about first aid kits for a minute? I mean, how many Bandaids does one family need? I am certain when we first purged our bathroom, 60% of what was thrown out were random items that would've only been used had some insanely bloody medical emergency occurred in our living room. I mean, wow.

Friends, have a medical kit. I applaud your Boy Scout preparedness. But consider sticking to what comes in the kit or will fit on one shelf in the medicine cabinet and pitch the rest. Besides, peroxide from 1984 is probably some kind of health hazard.

5. Holiday Decor

While you will often see the adorable Christmas lights or happy hauntings of decorated simple spaces online, most people focused on living simply opt out of storing a basement full of holiday decorative items.

This doesn't mean you can't be festive. It just means whatever you choose, like most things when living simply, they should have multiple duties whenever possible. This means white Christmas lights could function to brighten up a bedroom during the off-season and then to highlight a tabletop tree during the holidays.

You will undoubtedly find the longer you live simply, the more creative you'll get. This doesn't mean you have to give everything up. Instead, it means you are able to enjoy every single thing inside your home with intention and the knowledge that each item is truly functional while bringing you joy.

Chapter 8
Simplicity's Benefit for Mental Health

"When you are overwhelmed, tired, or stressed, the solution is almost always less. Get rid of something. Lots of somethings."

-Be More With Less

"Clutter smothers; simplicity breathes."

-Terry Guillemets

"I literally feel so much better in my body and my mind after ditching unnecessary stuff from our basement that I want to just walk through the space we made because having it organized feels so good."

-Sheila Hansen, Sheila Hansen CPA

My husband and I's decision to drastically downsize, give away more than 80 percent of our possessions, and sell our 15-acre farm in exchange for a 36-foot fifth wheel was motivated not by insanity but by years of research that supported the idea that a more simplified way of life can promote better behavior and more opportunity for success for kids with anxiety and behavior diagnoses like our son's.

It is possible to encourage positive responses and depress feelings of anxiety in you or your extreme child by taking some simple steps to declutter and downsize your stuff. Simplified living has benefits beyond creating a more organized space.

Here are your **Five Rules for Improving Mental Health through Simplified Living**.

1. Less Stimulation for Sensory Overload

Behavior meltdowns happen in the face of a sensory challenge or when our son feels incapable of articulating a feeling or emotion. The result? An explosion of emotion. It seems simple, but removing the sources of sensory overstimulation can relieve this anxiety.

Picture the traditional child's bedroom: a brightly colored cartoon-character bedspread, pictures of action heroes on the walls, bins overflowing with toys that make sounds or light up. Maybe there is a canopy or an extra decorative pillow array. Perhaps there are LEGOs, hundreds of them, scattered around across a rug that looks like a town. Its texture is scratchy.

Just the bedroom alone, nevermind other rooms in the home or an additional playroom, harbors untold sensory overstimulation.

Downsizing all of that "stuff" has diminished the sensory overload for our son. He and our daughter each use their two square fabric bins. If a toy doesn't fit, it doesn't stay. So, they each have one bin for stuffed animals and the other for dolls or action figures, racecars, or a wooden kitchen set. This reduces the drive to choose between so many things, and have access to a million different stimuli all at once. Their room is decorated with calming colors and simple decor. They share a bookshelf and a desk, and that is it.

Neither child has ever complained that it isn't enough, and the sensory reduction has been a huge assist for our son's needs.

2. More Intentional and Quality Time to Increase Happiness

Our kids don't want mountains of stuff from us. They just want *us*. Drastically downsizing all of the things I had to clean, keep up with, fold, and take care of has afforded us many more hours together.

And spending less money on stuff means we can afford to take more trips and engage in adventures like playing outside, going fishing, and teaching each other new things. Before simplifying our lifestyle, we let our son cook with us twice. Now, he loves to learn by measuring ingredients, making shopping lists, or chopping vegetables (After having learned knife safety, of course! Thanks for checking, Karen.).

Simplification has increased how much quality time we spend together as a family which has made us happier and more content.

3. Reduced Stress and Anxiety

I have anxiety and I raise a child with anxiety. Trust me, friend, we drive the Crazy Train most days.

However, choosing this simple way of living allows me to take time to breathe instead of stressing over an endless to-do list. We can clean our entire house each weekend in less than an hour. Less stuff, less square footage, less stress and anxiety.

Parenting a child with anxiety is a tricky road to navigate because you can't possibly predict all of his emotional triggers. Additionally, when your child has other diagnoses, such as ADHD or ASD, he tends to have anxiety because of his primary diagnosis.

Will kids like me? Will I make friends? Will they play fair on the playground?

The list is a mile long.

Simplification has allowed us to be a one-income family. That means one of us stays home to Roadschool our kiddos so our son can learn at his own pace. No more anxiety about school. That is maybe the best thing ever.

Johanna Elsner, co-owner and designer at Perch and Nest Tiny Homes and mother of two including her rockstar daughter who happens to use a wheelchair adds, "If it's not life or death, finish the task at hand before entertaining any interruptions. In our home, this means I will finish unloading the dishwasher before I come to your room to get a stack of books off the shelf or finish a phone call before setting up a craft project. This has become a house rule that has not only saved my sanity, but also taught our daughter patience and understanding with a caregiver."

Sometimes choosing simplicity and joy means teaching ourselves and others to take a breath, step back, and find a new strategy or approach.

4. Appreciate Simplicity

In the age of excess screen time, birthday parties with bounce houses, and extravagant summer vacations, kids have a lot competing for their attention, and parents feel pressured to keep up. Simplifying our lives and downsizing our stuff has taught us some pretty beautiful lessons through our kids.

Our 7-year-old son didn't know what an iPad was until recently. Our daughter would hands-down choose playing in the dirt over watching TV, and both of our kids have spent more hours in a $10 inflatable pool in our yard than they have on any vacation in their lifetime.

You know what? They love it!

They love running around outside together playing hide and seek as much as I used to love riding bikes and climbing trees until the streetlights came on. It is a simpler way of living, and it is teaching them to use creativity, imagination, and problem solving to dream up awesome adventures! It also reminds us, as parents, to slow down and enjoy simple things like them playing in the dirt or taking a walk instead of feeling like we have to constantly entertain our kids.

5. Focus on Generosity

We get asked often about the best part of going tiny or living simply with our kids. I honestly love having the time to model kindness, and implement it with my kids because we no longer work so many hours that giving back seems more like exhaustion than generosity.

When I taught at the second chance high school last year, my students—ages 16-21—became like big brothers and sisters to my kids. Our little family was able to serve these students who battled homelessness, addiction, and family crisis.

We were able to feed them, clothe them, and just spend genuine time together.

Y'all don't know the number of tears I have cried over the opportunity that season in our lives brought to our family—both joyful and sad tears.

Children can be taught how to hate or how to love relentlessly. We chose love.

Every time our kids count out their toys and cut that number in half to give away, they learn the joy of blessing someone who has less than they do. The importance they once placed on 'stuff' lessens with each purge. They are teaching others and reminding us what being kind looks like—and that is a beautiful illustration I hope I never forget.

The benefits of living simply are endless, but the improvements to your mental health can be immeasurable. With the simple reduction of clutter, increased organization, less cleaning time, and more focus on being intentional, we are finally able to thrive as the best version of ourselves.

Chapter 9
When People Think You're Weird

*"Minimalism isn't about what you own.
It is about why you own it."*

-Brian Gardner

*"Regardless of what you choose to do, life never
offers any guarantees. Take calculated risks.
Be more available. Spend your time wisely. Make
your life less about things and more about living."*

-Chris Schapdick, *Tiny Industrial*

*"Some birds' feathers are too bright to be caged. I
know I'm not that colorful but a bird just the same."*

-Old Crow Medicine Show, *Wagon Wheel*

Even though I hope you feel like we are friends by
now (I've already planned our next coffee date), I
have no way of knowing how old you are. Since

turning 30, I generally assume everyone is younger than me. As you age, most people begin to care less about what others think about them. Of course, that is a generality.

I have never cared what people think. In fact, I actually thrive on people's adverse reactions when I insist on choosing to do whatever is most opposite of popular. One of my most favorite memories is when my husband proposed to me on a rock climbing trip in a place he knew I thought was the most beautiful—but he didn't have a ring. So, naturally, he improvised by buying a $2.00 mood ring at the tiny Kentucky farmer's market in the mountains where we had camped.

Y'all I *love* that ring and still have it 13 years later. I loved even more the looks on people's faces when their reaction was, "Oh! Show me the ring!" and I whipped out that dime store hunk of color-changing metal. I still laugh thinking about the looks of shock and awe.

Regardless of how much I might intentionally do things to freak people out because their reaction insights hilarity and not self-doubt or panic, I do care about the feelings of those I love.

Among the most common things I hear from people considering downsizing or living simply as I travel and speak about simple living with kids are comments like, "Our parents aren't supportive," or, "Our friends think we are insane."

Lean in close for this one, friends. You *are* crazy.

I mean, it's a brilliant kind of crazy, but when you intentionally choose to live your life completely against what we've grown up learning as the status-quo, you can expect to ruffle some feathers. Some of those birds are generational and they still assume everyone who goes to college gets a great paying job the second they graduate and is happy for all eternity. Well, my English and Biblical Studies major and I are here to disprove that theory HARD.

Instead of considering how your decision to simplify life affects others, begin by looking inward. Here are **Five Questions for When People Think You're Weird.**

1. What are Your Fears?

Sometimes we think we are afraid of something but the root cause of our fear is not what we thought. That fear can paralyze us if we aren't intentional about acknowledging it.

Do you think you are afraid you won't be able to be the hostess you enjoy being if you live in a more simplified space with fewer things or even a smaller house?

Many people live in tiny homes like us and still host gatherings, throw parties, and even have kids stay overnight. The root of the fear isn't that you can't host a successful party, but rather that people might not come if your space is smaller or your stuff is reduced.

Friends, the Karens of the world will still hate. It's what they do. I decided to let them be miserable a long time ago and I'd just leave them to it. Afterall, they are professionals.

Not only will people still come to your rockin' parties, but they will actually enjoy each other more in a cozy space with fewer distractions. It is easier to prepare a small area with less decor and takes less time to clean up. Everybody wins (Except Karen. She sucks.)!

2. What are Your Motivators?

Are you looking to simplify your way of living to reduce debt, prevent clutter, and decrease stress and chaos? All of those are valid reasons. Identify yours and keep them at the forefront.

I use sticky notes.

It may partially be my affinity for office supplies mixed with my innate sense of forgetfulness, but I love to put a goal or a motivator on a brightly-colored sticky and slap that puppy in a predominant place so I am likely to be reminded of it's message daily.

Having these reminders of our "why" will help us stay focused and centred on aligning our lifestyle with our end goal, especially when Karen starts running her judgy trap.

3. What are *Their* Fears?

It's a generality, sure, but most people who are unsupportive of an idea that seems against the grain are just unsure about how it will affect *them*.

Some may be worried about logistics or practical things if it is your mom or your uncle Roy who always reminds you to check your oil before a long trip. Try to be mindful that these people may just be worried for you. Being understanding can go a long way to alleviate their fears.

Don't allow others to project their fears, which can come out as anger or disapproval, onto you and affect your decision to simplify.

4. What are *Their* Motivators?

Much like how our moms told us boys only picked on us in elementary school because they actually had a crush on us, people who are mean and judgy are usually hurting.

So, ask yourself, what is Karen's actual deal?

Are the people in your life who think you choosing to minimize your stuff, give unnecessary items away, and even trade gift-giving for experiences just secretly wishing they had the guts to do the same? Are they afraid you'll be successful and become wildly happy while they eat cheese balls and watch *Roseanne* episodes and you are off chasing your dreams?

Don't hate them for being afraid. You were once, too, remember?

The key is to remind them that you are happy to hear them out, but it is your decision and it is what is best for you *right now*. I tell people often that this is the best fit for our family *right now*. Should it not become the best fit, then we will course-correct and make necessary changes.

> Friends, we just need to stop letting other
> people's opinions drive our decisions.
> They aren't responsible for our happiness.

5. Remember Your *WHY*.

> No matter what happens on this journey
> towards simplicity, always remember your *why.*

For many people, debt or clutter, career change, or chaos may be the primary motivator for wanting to breathe long enough to simplify so they can actually begin to enjoy life again.

As usual, I am different. When I started speaking at simple living events and writing for tiny house builders and folks in the industry, it was a side hustle. It was a few gigs to bring in extra cash for a teacher who was struggling to make it for her one income family. But I knew that industry wasn't the end for me.

I love the tiny house movement, don't get me wrong. But my *why* is my kids.

Being an extreme parent and raising a child with invisible disabilities and a mental health diagnoses will change your life forever. It is both the hardest and most beautiful job I'll ever have. That is why I talk about our son every single chance I get. Because *he* is my why. He is why we went tiny— to provide opportunities for his needs to be met, to better parent him, and to Roadschool he and his sister so he wouldn't become another labeled kid in public school, but instead to foster a love of learning how he learns best.

Friends, never, ever forget your why. I promise it will begin to take center stage and, eventually, you won't even hear Karen anymore.

Chapter 10

How Simple Living Saves You Money

"Be content with what you have; rejoice in the way things are. When you realize there is nothing lacking, the whole world belongs to you."

-Lao Tzu

"Minimalism isn't about what you don't have. Just the opposite. It's about what you now have."

-Andrew Odom

When we decided to simplify, financial freedom was one of our driving motivators. Ours was a hard-working family who still lived paycheck to paycheck due to circumstances like medical bills and living in areas of high poverty and low employment where the living wage was well below the national average.

Since simplifying, we have been able to pay off a significant portion of our pre-existing debt. We have also been able to build a savings that is allowing us to both travel for the first time since having kids, and to experience the freedom that comes without worrying when the next payday will arrive. It is extra meaningful because now our paychecks come from jobs we sincerely love.

So, here is a list of the **Five Rules Of Saving Money with Simplified Living**.

1. Watch Cash Leave Your Hand

Since being budget conscious by choice instead of necessity, our perspective has changed. It is pretty amazing what kind of turnaround happens when you pay cash for all things outside of automatic online bill payments.

When I have to physically watch Karen at the gas station take the $10 bill out of my icy cold grip in exchange for a bottled water and a bag of SunChips, friends, I seriously reconsider my snack choices! Paying cash helps to keep tight control of unnecessary expenditures as well as allows you the freedom to save up money without having it show up in your account to be spent on things like groceries or gas.

2. Aim to Beat Your Budget

Once you get in the habit of creating a monthly budget (it takes a while, just like any habit), you will be able to track how much money you have coming in and how much you have going out in various categories each month. This allows you to adjust line items each month, based on previous spending and saving.

Maybe it's because I am competitive, but this has driven my husband and me to compete for who can save the most/spend the least. We also try to spend less than the other in certain monthly expense categories, such as couponing for groceries. We save by knowing what we will spend eating out and can sometimes add another trip or two by using apps that accrue rewards or even intentionally choosing nights at restaurants where kids eat free.

3. More Money Doesn't Have To Equal More Spending

When you live simply, you generally keep what you need from your original purge. However, if things come up or something that you want goes on sale, you should have a miscellaneous budget item or cash savings. This should be a built-in part of your monthly financial plan.

4. Seek Savings from Adventure

With a growing number of kids prone to hours sitting in front of the computer or tablet, the idea of playing outside is almost becoming a thing of the past. However, those who are actively choosing to challenge the status-quo for everything from income margins to housing expense and environmental impact are turning the ideas of staying cooped up on its end.

As the number of people choosing to live simply increases, this population is experiencing some pretty incredible results that come only from spending more time outdoors and less time inside. Simple living encourages you to spend more time doing things outside—and you remember why you gleaned so much joy from outdoor play as a child.

Your teen can still text an impressively startling 67,000 abbreviated characters and emojis per minute while sitting outside or going on a walk. I listen to audiobooks in my hammock (because...kids) so I can enjoy the breeze and soak up some vitamin D. It is a win-win.

Many local parks and recreation areas have outdoors adventure items such as bikes, kayaks, paddle boards, and even overnight camping equipment for free or a very inexpensive rental fee. They exist to promote fun in the outdoors. It costs next to nothing and can create a mountain of memories for your family without having to buy and store a ton of gear.

5. Use Less, Spend Less

One of the biggest changes we made in our journey toward simple living is going down to one car for a year. Truthfully, I didn't think it was possible. We had two kids, both involved in activities and my husband and I both worked. I can now say with confidence that it was one of the best things we've ever done.

Reducing in such a drastic way not only saved us money on gas, maintenance, and upkeep, but it brought us closer together and provided more time to be a family while encouraging us to slow down and learn to say no to some things that really only served to stress us out. Instead of one of us going the opposite direction of the other, we went together.

In addition to less spending on our cars, with less clothing, we have less to launder. This meant we opted to sell our bulky washer and dryer and get a hand-crank model. Before I lose some of you here, I was *very* skeptical. I told my husband he was insane for suggesting it and that my idea of a pioneer woman stopped far before hand crank appliances.

However, now that we've used it for a year, I'll admit he was right. Our water and electric bills are reduced, our clothes smell awesome from line-drying, and our severely ADHD son has a chore he takes pride in accomplishing, all while using his extra energy when it is warm outside.

Not all of these suggestions may be viable options for your living situation, however, I'd challenge you to implement one for a month. Instead of selling a vehicle, try being a one-car family for 30 days to see if you can swing it. If you can, that is one less payment, gas fill-up, and oil change you have to worry about. Implementing practical steps toward simple living can provide major savings in the long run.

Chapter 11
What To Do If Simplicity Scares You

"You don't need more things to make your home beautiful. You need less things distracting you from what's already there and beautiful."

-The Bottom Line Mom

"Too many people spend money they haven't earned to buy things they don't want, to impress people they don't like."

-Author Unknown

Simple living can be modified to suit everyone's individual needs. Purging your closets and countertops of unwanted and unnecessary stacks of *stuff* is not only good for your household but great for your soul.

Clutter encourages anxiety.

So, even if simplifying seems overwhelming, there are steps you can take toward becoming less chaotic and more organized without giving away most of what you own.

My planner may be color-coded, but sometimes my house isn't. So, here are some simple ways even the messiest can become a minimalist.

~~Five~~ Nine Rules to Super Simply Simplify

1. Start with One Room at a Time

Right after Christmas, even though we live in 300 square feet, I felt like I couldn't look somewhere where there wasn't a stack of something about to attack me. I felt like I was about to be recommended for an episode of *Hoarders*. So, I started with my pantry. No, it didn't help with the piles of Christmas gifts and the graveyard of wrapping paper, but it was a small area I could easily control. Once I finished that, the feeling of accomplishment was motivation to move on to something bigger.

2. If You Don't *Love* It, It Has to Go

This was the mantra in our house before downsizing. Some studies suggest (enter Marie Kondo and her sweet little self) holding each item of clothing or trinket from your bookshelf in your hand and if it doesn't bring joy or trigger a positive memory, it has to go.

We are now left with only the things that have deep meaning for us or clothes and shoes that sincerely make us feel good.

As a woman of solid size, this one is hard. *But what if I lose weight?* Or *What if I gain some back?*

I like to be prepared. However, some of us are hanging on to our pre-teen N*SYNC concert t-shirt and, sister, that reunion tour ain't happening! We need to move on.

So, go through your closet, dresser drawers, shoe racks, and handbag holders, and throw out or donate everything you haven't worn in the last year (six months is actually preferable). I promise you will be shocked at how many items this eliminates if we are truly honest with ourselves.

3. Make Piles

This gets easier the more you do it, trust me. Once you start throwing things into boxes (labeled: Keep, Donate, and Trash), you get on a roll and it is so freeing to let things go. It feels great to donate to those who need the clothes you haven't fit into since high school, and then you have space in your closet for things you actually feel comfortable wearing.

Be sure not to let the boxes sit around cluttering up your space. Take them where they were designated and wash your hands of what you let go.

4. Make a Cleaning Schedule on Rotation

Once you've cleared out and decluttered, make yourself an easy-to-follow schedule that rotates rooms in your house. Beyond your typical laundry and cleaning up leftovers, it will keep you from becoming overwhelmed to know that on Mondays you clean the bathrooms and on Wednesdays you straighten the living room. No more weekends filled with stress from a house that looks like hurricane Katrina hit and you did nothing to recoup the damages.

We like to get our kids involved. Our 7-year-old is an expert at taking out the trash and vacuuming and our almost 3-year-old loves to unload the dirty and clean laundry baskets. These simple tasks teach them responsibility and help them feel like they are contributing to the family chores while leaving you one less to-do.

5. Rid Yourself of Expired Items

I have no explanation as to why many of us shop and hold onto pantry items like we are living through the Great Depression, but Karen, this isn't 1930, girl! Even folks like me who know the struggle of Ramen noodles and paycheck-to-paycheck living can usually afford to replace the ranch dressing they've had open in their fridge since New Kids on The Block were actually new.

Many women have makeup that used to line the shelves of our 8th grade Caboodle case and hair accessories we haven't worn since our headbands were hand-decorated with puffy paint. *WHY!?* Friends, can we have a collective trash bag frenzy, please!?

If it is out of date, it needs to go in your Trash box and then keep it moving.

6. Buy Quality Over Quantity

Okay, admittedly, this one might hurt a little at first but you have to trust me on this. When you cut your closet contents in half (or, in our case, by 80 percent), you want to sincerely love the things that remain. This means when you buy a new item, you not only remove an old one, but you should also be buying things that will last.

I was just able to replace three mediocre sweaters with one from Patagonia that I really love and is versatile enough to wear traveling or to the office. The initial cost on these items seem higher, but when you can get 10+ years of wear out of them, your investment was well worth it the price.

7. Invest in Items with More than One Use

This is a simple living mantra. That is why you've read it over and over in this book. If it only has one use, you don't need it. We need a coffee pot that doubles as a hot water maker for tea, a can opener that opens bottles of wine and beer, and a table that is also a prep space and desk.

If you look at buying items, especially the larger purchases for your home, as needing to be multifunctional, you will spend less money and have less stuff.

8. For Everything, There Is A Place

This is the main culprit of cleanliness-related mom anxiety. Why must we have piles of hair ties, a collection of LEGOs, and a mountain of bills and junk mail covering our countertops? For the love of organization, Throw. It. Out!

A clean counter in your kitchen will provide endless happiness for mom and sends all of the unwanted treasures usually found there to their rightful locations. Then, if Suzy can't wear a ponytail Monday or Johnny's LEGO truck only has three wheels, they might begin to learn to pick up after themselves.

Whether you live in a tiny house or a mansion, there should be some sort of order. Our kids know they each have two toy bins. If new toys won't fit, they have to rid themselves of enough old ones to make room, or they have a choice to make.

My husband and I know our wall-mounted mail holder will only hold so much, so eventually, we will have to go through it, separate it, and pay bills or respond to mail. In our old, larger home, mail would pile up, collect dust, and remain unopened.

This same rule should apply for kitchen items, pantry food, tools and gardening, and everything else one might keep in or around the home.

9. Some Things Are More Worth Your Money Than Your Time

This is an important step and one I am continuing to learn. Whether you are a traveling single or a settled family, a retiree, or a divorcee starting over, you have responsibilities. Sometimes our time is worth more than our money.

This means, instead of stressing over the heart-wrenching fact that you honestly cannot keep up with your family's laundry on top of a full-time job, motherhood, being a wife, and the everyday of running a household, it might be a worthwhile investment to pay a dry cleaner to launder your clothes or a housekeeper to clean toilets. There is no shame in that, sister! It isn't defeat. It is working smarter, not harder.

No matter what your initial fears are surrounding simple living, don't let them keep you from a life that is less overwhelming and filled with more joy. Friends, many people assume you *have* to live with debt, or that *everyone* is stressed out. To some degree, that is our own choice.

So start now and take steps—no matter how small— toward living simply and reclaiming your joy.

Chapter 12
Life Lessons from Living Simply

*"Edit your life frequently and ruthlessly.
It's your masterpiece after all."*

- Author Unknown

After embracing the joy that comes from simple living, you begin learning things about yourself, your loved ones, and the world. It is almost like the absence of all of the *extra* allows you to see more clearly, as if having less provides a better view of people and things.

Here are a few life lessons learned by living simply.

1. You Can Do Hard Things

Downsizing our house was one thing, but when we were considering going to a shared vehicle, even *I* thought we had lost our minds. I mean, how were we possibly going to be able to get me to work, the kids to all the things, my husband to work three evenings a week, plus his MMA class, plus the rec center, *and* simple things like groceries or the post office?!

It can't be done, I rationalized.

But we did it. And it was pretty awesome.

My husband and I have been together for 13 years, four houses, a townhome, two family members' basements, two kids, countless jobs, and we've always had at least two vehicles, sometimes three. We'd never wanted or needed to go somewhere and not had the option to just get in a car and go.

The idea of having only one shared vehicle had me feeling all panicky and trapped.

But what if this one breaks down?!

What if one of the kids gets hurt but I have the car at work?

What if you need to take them to co-op but we forgot and the car isn't at home!?

I named off a laundry list of reasons why I had rationalized that it wouldn't work, but we did it anyway. And guess what? We lived through it.

We saved thousands of dollars in that year on oil changes, gas fill ups, tires and repairs. We became a closer family who wasn't afraid to ask for help when we needed the car for something. We depended on each other even if it meant getting up waaaayyyy before the sun to drop me off at the airport or to take someone to an appointment.

If we hadn't tried, we'd never have known and we'd never have reaped the benefits of it. It was hard, but we did it—together.

2. Don't Make Fear-Based Decisions

If I never went after a dream or a goal when I was afraid of the risk, I'd have never accomplished anything.

In talking to thousands of people across the country who have aspirations of simplifying their lives, they all could list a hundred fears.

But what if there isn't enough space?

What if I need something I've gotten rid of in a purge?

What if people think we are crazy?

Where will guests sleep if they visit?

We could build a community out of what-ifs, but the common thread among those of us who have taken the plunge is that it's one of the best decisions we've ever made.

Don't let fear guide your decision making or you'll be left with nothing to show for it but regret.

3. Presence Over Presents

We have never been the type of parents who buy our kids a lot of toys and things, but because both sides of our families are large, it is easy for us to bring a car load of toys home after a birthday or Christmas. While we teach our kids to serve and give back, it just seemed like we were constantly giving away *things.*

We realized this had to be our children's decision and not ours. I was surprised by the freedom with which our kids cut things loose.

What we were experiencing was a freedom from things we thought we *needed.* I thought I *needed* to hold on to mementos from my past and our son thought he *needed* every little trinket and toy. My husband and I thought we *needed* time to unwind after work with a mindless TV show, but now we rarely even turn on the TV.

We are, however, making our own memories. We are experiencing our community, visiting new places, and being active together every chance we get. We are getting dirty, building things, learning things, and enjoying building our lives together in a big way.

Simple living is pretty incredible and costs next to nothing.

4. Intentionally Be Intentional

Admittedly, this is not my spiritual gift. Emotions make me clammy and uncomfortable. However, allowing myself to let go a little is kind of amazing.

Since simplifying, we have freed ourselves from the mundane but necessary parts of everyday life. We no longer have a yard to mow; a fence to fix; a barn to clean; a house to sanitize from a week of baby goo; or mountains of laundry to wash, forget about, rewash, smell to make sure we didn't leave it too long, then forget about folding in baskets for the upcoming week.

All of that is gone. What we are left with is ourselves and each other.

Our job now—our primary goal— is to be together and enjoy life.

I am able to focus so I can give my best to my husband and kids.

Now we can let ourselves have time to feel things, discuss things, and experience things we just couldn't or didn't make a priority before.

We are intentional about what we choose to eat, where we choose to visit, and what we teach our kids. Every decision can be intentional because we have freed up the *time* to make those choices on purpose.

I still don't do it perfectly. However, we sit around the table together and we talk about school, our days, what we learned. We are intentional.

I can now read bedtime stories to my kids each night and kiss boo-boos and remind our son who struggles with his emotions that mama does, too, and that's okay. It is a change I may never have experienced otherwise.

Transition is never easy, but the liberation born from this type of simplicity is indescribably beautiful.

Chapter 13
Simplicity Moving Forward

"Billions of marketing dollars are aimed at your eyes at every moment to convince you of what you lack so you'll purchase a product. This feeds the fear that we do not have enough, that we are not enough. Turning off the noise and living in purposeful simplicity is nothing short of a revolutionary act of defiance."

-Carmen Shenk, Kitchen Simplicity

"Minimalism is asking why before you buy."

-Francine Jay

Friend! You did it! You threw out old food. You got rid of your hoardy stacks of mail on the counter. You pitched kitchen appliances from your wedding registry in 1983. You even found yourself parting with the box full of pre-pregnancy clothes and I could not be more proud!

Now that you are living in a clutter-free zone and feeling like you can take on the world, I want to remind you of your basic rules moving forward in this crazy awesome life of simplicity, because even we rockstars slip a little sometimes.

Here are your **Five Rules of Living Simply** from here forward.

1. 50 Items, Per Person, Per Season

Aside from our off-season or next-size-up tote for kids, we agreed on 50 items per person in your home, per season you experience wherever you live most often. That means if you live year-round in Texas where it never drops below 60 degrees, you might have a few more than 50 items since they are all the same season. Those of us in the north will have our fall/winter tote and our spring/summer tote.

2. Think Twice Before You Buy

This rule can be summed up in a few bullet points of its own:

- Will you use/wear it more than once?

- Does it serve more than one purpose?

- Can you borrow/rent it and then return it instead of buying?

- Can it be replaced with an experience?

- Sleep on it.

Most things that seem like a great idea in the moment are actually things we stand to regret later. So take five minutes to answer these quick questions before you buy something new and, whenever possible, sleep on it so you can wake up clear-headed and without the item in your hand at Target.

3. New In, Old Out

Whenever you are considering buying something new, remember that something you already own must be replaced.

Settle yourself, Karen. I am not saying you have to throw out a perfectly good can of green beans because you forgot you hadn't used them yet and accidentally bought another one. This isn't Guantanamo.

This rule applies to shoes, clothing, and larger items such as kitchen and bath necessities, bedding, appliances, and electronics. In order to bring in something new, something already owned must be donated or tossed.

**Remember, with simplicity,
there is no room for clutter.**

4. Implement a Library System

Possibly my favorite rule: implement a library system. This can be for your kids toys as I mentioned before with a bin of things they keep with a relative and trade items out whenever they visit. It could also be for the hobby item you enjoy most such as books, paints, fishing gear, or biking.

Keep your off-season or extra things somewhere you won't frequent so you learn what you really use often. Then you can trade things out whenever you visit that storage location without taking up added space in your simple living area.

5. Purge Every Six Weeks

After living tiny for nearly two years, we still religiously purge every 6-8 weeks. This means, regardless of our square footage, we go through clothes, shoes, accessories, dishes and kitchen items, and anything we generally keep stored outside. If we haven't used it or worn it since the last purge, it has to go.

This rotation of things keeps the items at home fresh while maintaining the integrity of simple living. No room for disorder and chaos.

Friends, I follow the rules I've set for simplified living because I am constantly focused on my *why*.

After our little family had endured nearly three years of hardship raising an explosive child, crippled by the paralyzing fear and isolation that accompanies parenting extreme children lead me to grow tired of the chaos and crazy of a mundane existence.

After our son's initial diagnosis (he has five now) I spent a year researching how my husband and I could give him every opportunity to succeed in knowing the challenges he'd likely face. As a public educator and person who has over 20 years experience working with people with varying disabilities, I knew our son would face obstacles, but we kept coming back to the same conclusion: simplify.

So, we got rid of over 80 percent of our belongings, sold our house and 15 acres, and one of our vehicles—and bought a 36-foot fifth wheel which we've now lived in for nearly two years. It has afforded us the freedom to be a one-income family so we can Roadschool our son, and he is excelling. He loves the hands-on learning and the ability to go at his pace, be it more advanced than his state-assigned grade level, or more slowly in subjects he doesn't enjoy.

Our life seems crazy to many onlookers, but we are just a regular family doing everything in our power to allow our children to excel academically, to experience culture, to go on adventures, and to live a life of joy.

As our parenthood evolved into simplified living and eventually tiny house living in order to better meet our son's needs, the idea for this book was born.

And here you are.

Your *why* likely doesn't match mine and that's okay. Whatever brought you to this aisle of your local bookstore or on this page of Amazon late at night while you were busy not sleeping, I am grateful.

Let this be your landing page, your library of resources, of painful discovery, and wild learning. This is your place to research and read about one mama's journey and what she is learning along the way. This is your first stop on a road toward freedom.

This is the ability to unbury yourself from the chaos and crazy—and instead, to choose joy.

Acknowledgements

To my tribe. You know who you are and you are the fiercest bunch of wonderful and the most perfect brand of crazy for me. I am so grateful for each of you helping me not be the conductor of the crazy train!

About the Author

Brynn is the creator of The Mama on the Rocks. She is a writer, speaker, and coach to parents of extreme children, fellow and future Roadschoolers, and folks looking to simplify their lives to reclaim the joy-filled journey we're meant to live!

Brynn has 20 years of experience working with people with mental health diagnoses and both physical and mental disabilities. Her expertise and research in the field peaked when her own son began exhibiting signs of behavior disorders in 2012.

She and her husband sold their farm to live tiny in 2017 in order to better meet the needs of their extreme child and since then have been Roadschooling their kids and traveling for speaking events about the benefits for mental health and joy in living simply while chasing a life of adventure.

Since then, Brynn has created eCourses, spoken at conferences, and taught educators, professionals, and parents throughout the country about how to raise extreme children and how to differentiate for them within a classroom environment. She has spoken throughout the US at events surrounding simple living and why it is possible for everyone, no matter the size of their home.

Made in the USA
Coppell, TX
01 May 2021